The Natural Guitar

Ron Prellop

CONTENTS

AUTHOR'S NOTE 1

START HERE 3

SOME REALLY BASIC ADVICE 4

HOW TO USE THIS BOOK 5

HOW LONG WILL IT TAKE? 5

GUITARS 6

AMPS AND OTHER GEAR 7

FINGERPICKING VS. FLATPICKING 8

METRONOMES 9

POSITIONS 9

HOW TO PLAY 9

I WANT TO PLAY FAST! 11

LEVEL ONE: SURF'S UP! 14

THE SECRET: BREAKING THROUGH! 16

LEVEL TWO: HALF-BOXES 18

THE BIG KAHUNA! 18

THE OTHER SIDE 19

LEVEL THREE: THE RELATIVE 20

GROWING UP 21

REGROUPING 21

LEVEL FOUR: BUILD THE BRIDGE, THEN CROSS IT 22

LEVEL FIVE: FLIPPING IT OVER 25

CONGRATULATIONS! 26

LEVEL SIX: CROSSING THE BRIDGES 27

LEVEL SEVEN: HORIZONS BEYOND THE HORIZON 28

A FEW FAREWELL NOTES 31

AUTHOR'S NOTE:

Many out there will criticize this book for not teaching the usual guitar-playing content: chords, notation, tabs, intervals, triads, modes, etc. Yes, it's fine to learn those things, and that's absolutely cool, but that's not the purpose here. Read on.

Our focus is this: 99% of the guitars out there end up collecting dust in the closet, because their owners don't have the time or patience to learn to play them, or they're motivated, but go about learning the wrong way and end up frustrated, when after ten years, they still can't play anything beyond strumming three chords or plinking the first ten seconds of some rock song.

Are you one of these, or are you one of those people who wants to be able to pick up a guitar and just *play* it, for minutes or for hours, any time, any place, just for your own pleasure, just playing spontaneously, as naturally as breathing or walking?

That's where this book comes in.

The purpose of this book is exactly that: to *quickly* teach you how to just pick up a guitar and *play* it, in a relaxed, *natural* manner, for your own pleasure - in your living room, on the back porch, by a fire, out under a tree… any time, any place, for as long as you want.

I say "quickly" because we will be completely bypassing the usual technical content you see in a million "beginner guitar" books, thus saving a massive amount of learning time.

So, then, what will we do here? Just as a hammer and saw are simple, basic tools you can use to build a beautiful house, we will teach you some simple, basic tools you can use to generate infinite quantities of beautiful music. You will learn what they are and how to use them, and in a couple of weeks you can be turning heads down at the music store.

Later, if you want, you can still go on to learn specific styles like jazz, rock or blues, play in a band, learn chord theory, etc. and that's great! This will give you a good, solid foundation to build on. But if you just want to learn to relax and play and enjoy your guitar any time, any place, this book is for you!

Thanks for being here, and have fun!

Ron Prellop

START HERE

It seems like everybody wants to play the guitar at one time or another. Probably 999 out of every 1,000 people have owned a guitar at some point on their lives, but maybe 1 out of 1,000 ever got to the point of actually being able to play it.

Why does this happen? There are more reasons than we can go into here, but one very common reason is that so much of guitar playing seems complex and confusing. Over the centuries, tens of millions, maybe hundreds of millions, of would-be musicians have gone to the music store and bought a guitar, maybe picked up a couple of instruction books and checked some internet forums, took it home and tried to start playing, and then started seeing all this jargon about playing an 9sus7 over a diminished 13th, major 5ths, minor 5ths, diminished 5ths, augmented 5ths, flatted 5ths, intervals, triads, inversions, dorian modes, phyrigian modes, ionian modes, lydian modes, mixolydian modes....well, you get the picture. One popular book consists, from cover to cover, of over ten thousand chords. That's all it is, just page after page after page of chords. And of course it's highly recommended by"experts."

So after a few weeks, what happens? Typically, the guitar ends up back in its case and in the closet and never touched again, until it's time to sell it to help pay for new tires for the family car. That's why classified ads and pawn shops always seem to have more "used" guitars on hand than they know what to do with: people feel like they can never master the Mount Everest of material they've been told that they "need to know" in order to be a "good player." So before they even start, they give up.

You can't help but wonder how many of those people would have stayed with it if they used a more practical, enjoyable approach such as the one in this book. Before we get into it, let's look at some basic topics.

SOME REALLY BASIC ADVICE

As I just said, there are few other areas where there are more self-proclaimed "experts" than in guitar playing, especially on the internet. "On the internet, everybody is an expert." It seems like everybody thinks his guitar is the best kind to use, his strings are the best strings to buy, you must learn these chords and those chords, and his favorite band or player is the best that ever lived, and everything else is trash, and if you don't agree, you're an idiot, and you're an idiot for buying this book.

Don't get sucked into this! Do what *you* want. Learn from others, sure, but weigh everything you read or hear. Make your own place in the music world; you have as much a right as anyone to your place in the universe.

HOW TO USE THIS BOOK

Stevie Ray Vaughan. B. B. King. Jimi Hendrix. Eric Clapton. Jeff Beck. Carlos Santana. Van Halen. Eric Johnson. Jimmy Page. John McLaughlin. What do all these people have in common, besides being the Gods of Guitar? They depend very heavily, sometimes entirely, on one thing: the Pentatonic Scale. *"Oh, noooooo!!!"* many will complain; not another book on those pentatonic scales!!!

Make no mistake about it: if you want to be a decent guitar player along these lines, you can learn- or not learn - all kinds of skill sets: scales, chords, inversions, modes, intervals, arpeggios, harmonics... it's a long list. But there's one thing that's an "umbrella skill" you have to have, if you want to be a good player: not just knowing the pentatonics, but *how to play them*.

"But wait," you say: there are already a zillion books out there on "how to play them." Yes, that's true, but get this: the secret is not "how to play them." The secret is but *how you learn to play them*. And that's where this book, the only one of its kind, is going to take you.

At first, it looks easy. Hey, it's just a pattern on the fretboard, divided into these five nifty little "boxes." Just learn those five boxes and you're good to go. Piece of cake, right? Not quite. If it were that easy, we'd all have our names in that list up there.

Learning the pentatonics the *right* way, however, will unlock an enormous amount of musical potential you didn't even know you had. In fact, after your first two or three weeks, you could be turning heads in the music store. If you practice daily, your progress will be extremely rapid; in fact, after a month you will be somewhat shocked at the sounds coming from your fingers.

Do it all right, and you should master everything here within a couple of months. By then, using these techniques, you will be a superb guitarist, playing fast (or slow) and smooth, producing beautiful, flowing music, any time, any place, as long as you want, no matter what mood you're in.

This book is actually pretty short, but covers a great amount of learning. Go through it slowly, mastering the content one paragraph, one level at a time. Do not skip anything! That will be a fatal mistake. A single paragraph may contain only a couple of sentences, but take a week of practice to master. Now, don't be afraid of that word "master." None of this material is difficult. Let me repeat that: *none of this is difficult*! Each individual component of this approach is, in itself, so easy your dog could do it. It just requires that you play the material repeatedly until you can produce it consistently, without thinking about what you are doing. Each level of the book assumes you have mastered the previous level to that point. That's all you need to do.

HOW LONG WILL IT TAKE?

One of the most difficult parts of learning to play the guitar is patience. Everybody wants to learn that "hot lick" from their favorite artist and rip it out tomorrow. That's another reason so many guitars end up in the closet: people want to play like Joe Rocker and can't quite make it, never mind the fact that Joe Rocker has been playing all day, every day for 40 years. After all, it's BORING to sit there and go duh, duh, duh for months on end, "waiting to get better." But no matter how good a learning approach is, it still takes some time to get where you can just lean back, relax and play something. There are no short cuts, but there are quicker ways to get where you want to go!

That being said, I will lay the cards on the table and be honest with you: with the approach we're using here, if you're a *raw* beginner, you're probably looking at a couple of weeks of daily practice before you can smoothly make some simple licks. To really play some nice stuff all over the neck, if you faithfully practice an hour a day, you're probably looking a month or so. Seem like a long time? Not really. How long have you had your guitar? How long has it been in the closet? Six months? Two years? 20 years? Stay with it, and that two months will be over before you know it. Think of something you did two or three months ago. Now think, if you'd started at that time, today you'd be playing some really neat stuff.

This book will get right to the meat, and not spend a lot of time focusing on things like the types of guitars, playing positions, the different types of woods, pickups, cables, amplifiers, and so on. There are oceans of information on those topics already out there and freely available, but we will touch on them briefly as they relate to our objective.

GUITARS

You can use this approach with any guitar: electric, acoustic, even classical. Whatever floats your boat, although I recommend starting with an electric, for several reasons. Physically, an electric is probably the easiest to play, because of the lighter finger pressure that is used. That means you can learn and progress faster, and then transfer it to other kinds of guitars if you want.

It can be demoralizing to start with an steel-string acoustic and spend your first month just tolerating pain and building up callouses on your fingertips. Then when you go on vacation, you come back and the callouses have disappeared, and it's back to Square One. In contrast, you can fret notes on an electric with little more than the weight of your finger.

Secondly, electric guitars, amps and pedals provide a massive, almost infinite range of sounds and effects, which allows you to express a wider range of emotion and feeling in your playing, instead of just sitting there going twang, twang, thunk.

It doesn't have to be a high-dollar, expensive instrument, especially at first. But keep in mind that you can go *too* cheap. A junk guitar will have things like sharp edges on the frets, loose or non-functional knobs and plugs, and go out of tune every 30 seconds. Guitars in cheap "starter packages" are notorious for this. But whatever you buy, what's really important is that it's set up well. Frequently, the action, tuning and intonation are hopelessly out of whack in guitars fresh off the rack, regardless of price.

I've seen $100 guitars that played smooth as butter because they were set up well, and I've seen $5,000 high-end guitars that were so messed up that they were literally unplayable. I won't mention the brand names; too many lawyers out there. So no matter what you buy, the first thing you should do is take it to a good guitar mechanic for a "setup." Tell him to set it up "low and smooth," and allow about $50 - $75 for this when you shop for an instrument.

Just be sure the person who does your setup is the best you can find, not just your neighbor's buddy who "knows a lot about guitars."If you have to drive 100 miles to get a good setup, do it. In general, I've found the small, privately owned shop to have better guitar techs than the big, chain "guitar superstores," but I've seen good and bad techs in both. Ask around. Believe me when I say there is absolutely *zero* room for compromise here. Whatever setup you get, you're stuck with. *Get this done right*!

AMPS AND OTHER GEAR

We won't spend a lot of time talking about the universe of amps, pedals and other gear. At this point in your development as a player, just get a good single-speaker amp, preferably one with a single 12- inch speaker, and be sure it has a headphone jack. Some smaller ones even have 6-inch or 8-inch speakers, and even those will get loud enough for the neighbors to call the police on you, but the 12 will give you a thicker, richer sound that you will almost certainly enjoy more. If you live in an apartment, with typical poor apartment soundproofing, you may end up using a small amp and using headphones. Of course, if you're playing in a band or professionally, you'll want something bigger and louder, but heck, if you're playing at that level, you wouldn't be reading this book anyway. In fact, these days you really don't need an amp, if you're just playing for yourself or you're short on money! Now you can get, for about $100, what's called a "headphone amp." It's a little device you plug into the guitar's output jack. Then you plug headphones into the device and listen to yourself play. Some of these have dozens of special effects and different types of amps built-in, giving you a huge variety of sounds, all while practicing silently to anyone around you.

Get a middle or higher priced guitar cable. Cables really do make a difference, up to a point. Don't go buy that $75 "boutique" cable, but don't buy the cheapest, either.

A guitar stand is highly recommended; it keeps your guitar right there, ready to grab and play. But remember that if you keep your guitar on a stand, it can be damaged if it's knocked over by kids, pets, or your wife's vacuum cleaner. I personally keep mine on a stand next to the amp, ready to play. Sometimes I walk past the guitar and just grab it, play for 30 seconds, put it back on the stand and keep walking. That's hard to do if you have it all packed away. If space is limited, consider the little U-shaped holder you screw into the wall. These work great! So... this one is your call.

Warning: if you keep your guitar on a stand, *do not* sit it right under an A/C vent or drafty window or where direct sunlight will bake it from 1:00 to 4:00 p.m. every day.

Get used to having your guitar in perfect tune every time you play it, starting right now. There's no excuse not to these days, with so much cheap, simple tuning technology available. I use a simple "guitar tuner" app on my smartphone, which does a perfect job of tuning all 6 strings in about 30 seconds. There are all kinds of tuners out there, and now many amps have built-in tuners as well.

FINGERPICKING VS. FLATPICKING

This could be a major decision you will have to make, if you haven't made it already: play with your fingers, or play with a pick? I'm not going to push you one way or the other, except to say that I play with a pick, because it's always the same; it's never sore or tired. By very subtle manipulation of the pick, you can dramatically vary the sound of the note, much more than you can with the soft end of your finger. Of course, on the other hand, with your fingers, you can play more than one string at the same time, which is impossible with a pick.

Suffice it to say that there are a lot of top players out there who play(ed) primarily with picks: Jimmy Page, B.B. King, Jimi Hendrix, Eric Clapton, Buddy Guy, Yngwie Malmsteen, Eric Johnson, Stevie Ray Vaughan, Steve Vai, Eddie Van Halen, Carlos Santana, John McLaughlin, Randy Rhoads, Duane Allman, David Gilmour, Billy Gibbons... need I say more?

One more comment about picks: almost all of the above players use a heavier, thicker pick. Very thin, flexible picks that "snap" off the string can really interfere with your ability to play smoothly and feel the flavor of the note.

METRONOMES AND BEATS

A quick word here about metronomes, something most guitar books don't really get into (and we won't, either, except for this little blurb). Actually, it's not so much about metronomes specifically as it is about having *some* kind of steady rhythm to play to. This is critically important, especially for beginners.

Again, modern technology comes to the rescue. Not only can you buy nice electronic metronomes for $10, but there are many excellent "metronome" apps for computers and smartphones that are free to download. Some of these are really feature-rich, producing not just a repeating beat, but combinations of beats in different tempos, ¾ time, etc.

Better yet is an electronic keyboard. Most modern keyboards, even the cheaper ones, have dozens, sometimes hundreds, of built-in percussion lines of every imaginable music type. Playing with one of these is about as close as you can get to playing with a professional drummer sitting next to you! And now you can get all kinds of rhythm tracks on the Web, YouTube, on smartphone apps, etc. Metronome, computer, smartphone, keyboard, whatever... but use *something*. Get in the habit of playing to some kind of background rhythm; it'll make a huge difference in your playing, as well as your satisfaction.

POSITIONS

There's an important point to make about playing positions: find a good one and stay with it. It should be comfortable and relaxed. If you have to look at the fretboard, that's fine, don't believe these people who cry "never look at the fretboard!" Do what works for you.

Never look at the fretboard? Look at Chet Atkins, arguably the greatest player of all time, hunched over his guitar, his eyeballs almost touching the strings, or Andres Segovia or Stevie Ray Vaughan or BB King or Erick Johnson or almost any other top player.

The left hand should be completely relaxed, so the ONLY thing it's doing is fingering the notes. Never, *never* use the left hand to "support" the guitar or "hold it up."

But the important thing is to get a good, solid position where the neck is stable, and where you can move your left hand fingers all over it without bending your wrist. Find a favorite chair and set it up to use only for your guitar practice. Then always, always practice and play in that chair, in that position. Constantly changing positions can dramatically slow down your learning and progress.

HOW TO PLAY

What a strange topic: "How to Play." But seriously, there are a few things you have to do correctly right from the beginning, or it'll be like taking off on a road trip with a flat tire. Specifically, I'm talking about how to hold the pick and how to pluck the strings. If you don't do it right, you'll never be able to play smoothly and quickly, no matter how much you practice.

Mainly, we have to start with the source of the sound itself: holding the pick. Three things are crucial for fast, smooth playing, and I don't use the word "crucial" lightly. All three of these are crucial! First, hold the pick correctly. Don't "pinch" it between your thumb and fingertip. Hold it against the first joint of the forefinger with your thumb, like this:

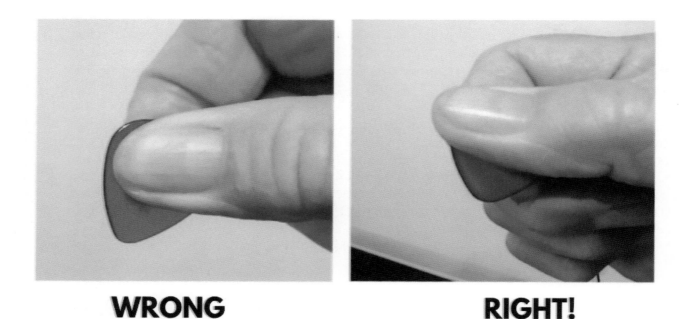

Second, stroke the string in astraight line, going slightly outward about 10 degrees on the downstroke, like this:

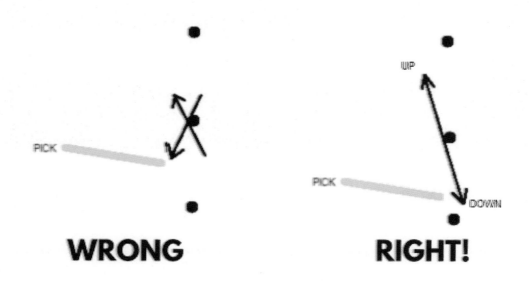

Third and last, hold the pick at a VERY slight angle to the string, causing the pick to slightly slide over the string, instead of "snagging" it:

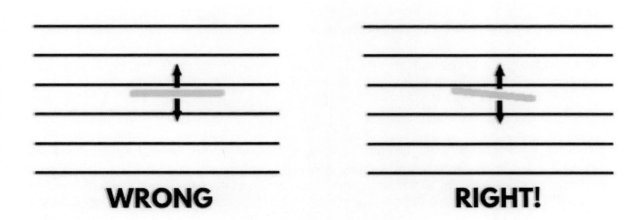

WRONG   **RIGHT!**

I WANT TO PLAY FAST!

One thing everybody wants to do, as soon as possible, is play fast, and that's another topic that has tsunami of "expert advice" on how to learn. The most common is to "play slow, then play fast." It's the old "walk before you can run" philosophy. Yes, there's some truth to that, but it still doesn't work for many people. So… are you ready? I'm going to tell you how to play fast, or rather, how to learn to play fast. Now, this is something you can work on while you're learning the other stuff in this book. So get ready, here it is.

First, remember that playing fast is a technique involving split-second timing and coordination between your two hands. So what you have to do is develop this technique, and once you do, you can use it all over the neck. Don't attempt to learn to play fast by practicing your favorite fast piece over and over, trying to play it faster and faster. It doesn't work. That's exactly what many people do, and then they get frustrated when after twenty years, they still can't play Stairway to Heaven or Texas Flood.

Second, review the other advice in this book about position, fingering, etc. because that's all part of it. Another element is your choice of a pick. Most big time player use a fairly stiff pick. A soft pick will "bend" slightly when you press it against the string, causing a slightly delay before the note is actually played. Also, use a pick made from a slippery material that will slide off the string easier. I personally love the "Heavy" weight Dunlop Gels; I "buff" the point a little on my pants leg to get it nice and slippery, and they work great, but there are many others out there. The important thing is for the pick to slightly slide over the string with as little resistance as possible.

OK, now let's get to the nitty-gritty on learning to play fast. There are four steps. Follow these steps,and you will learn to play fast, like you've always wanted!

Step one: find a repeatable selection of notes on the fingerboard. That is, one you can sort of "loop" without having to start over each time, that you can play up, then back down. It can just be a few notes. Just play those notes, going in both directions, smoothly, without stopping, keeping the up and down cadence of the pick.

Play them SLOWLY, with smoothness and perfection. DO NOT RUSH!!! Say two notes per second. Do this for a few hours, then you can speed up a little, say to 3 or 4 or 5 notes per second.

It's like pushing a car. If you start slowly, the car will gradually start to move, but if you throw yourself against it trying to make it move instantly, it will sit there, glued to the road, and won't budge. The exact same principle applies to learning to play an instrument. The faster you push it, the slower it goes!

Step two: keep playing this until you can do it unconsciously, *without thinking*. This is the critical point: to play at a good speed requires that you play unconsciously. You can not play fast and think about what notes to play at the same time! Your brain simply can't work that fast, and your fingers will slow down so your brain can keep up. Playing fast requires moving your technique from the conscious to the unconscious! This is the key!!!

So…. repeat your little pattern until you're playing it unconsciously, which frees your conscious mind to do other things, which takes us to the final step:

Step three: practice your unconscious playing everyday. Do it while you're watching TV, for example, or having a conversation. Again, you're playing unconsciously; you don't even realize you're doing it. Do this every day. Over time, the speed you want will come to you, like a flower growing out of the ground, a little more each day or week or month. This is how it's done!

Step four: hey, wait…. I said four steps, right? The fourth step is sort of an umbrella step: just be a guitar player. By that, I mean play a lot, practice a lot, practice seriously, with focus, don't just sit on the edge of the bed a couple of times a week and noodle. Don't just be "somebody who has a guitar." Make your decision! *Be a guitar player! The more you play, the faster you will build up speed!*

LEVEL ONE: SURF'S UP!

OK, let's get started. Earlier, we talked about the "pentatonic scale," and how everybody and his dog plays it, which is true to some extent. And we talked about how some of you may be rolling your eyes and groaning, "oh, nooooo, not another idiot talking about the pentatonic scale!" Some of you may have already learned some pentatonic patterns or "boxes" and are bored with just going duh, duh, duh in the same old "pentatonic box." You may be thinking if you hear the word "pentatonic" one more time, you're going to run out the front door screaming.

But see, it really doesn't work like that. As we said in the beginning, it's not the pentatonic scale that makes the music, it's how you *use* the pentatonic scale to make the music. And that's what this book does: it teaches you how to use the pentatonic scale in a free, spontaneous, creative manner. So please, please stay with us here. We're going places you've never been before. Yes, like a zillion other books, we'll focus on the pentatonic scale, but we'll learn how to use it like a carpenter uses a hammer and saw to build a mansion, or like an artist uses a paintbrush to paint a landscape.

One final comment: plan on spending at least three weeks on this section, longer if you practice less than an hour a day. This level contains some very, very fundamental concepts that you will carry with you for the rest of your guitar-playing life. Virtually *everything* is based on the content of *this* chapter.

OK, here we go. Don't grab your guitar yet, but have it tuned up, plugged in and ready to go, because we're going to play it in just a second. First, look at Figure 1 below. Blow it up bigger if you need to, that can help. See those brown dots? That's the E minor pentatonic scale. That's where we're going to start.

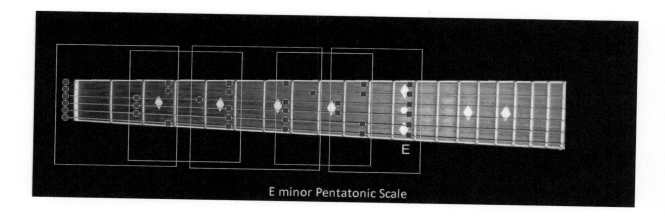

E minor Pentatonic Scale

Important point: notice how the dots go all the way across at the 12th fret. That's because the 12th fret is the same as the nut - "fret zero" - the open strings. Remember that any scale or pattern will repeat itself after the 12th fret. Think of the 13th fret as being the same as the 1st fret, only up higher on the neck.

Now let's go ahead and see it with all the dots. Look closely. See how the pattern repeats itself after the 12th fret?

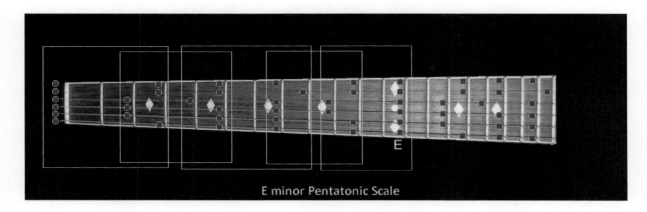

E minor Pentatonic Scale

Again, we call this the "E minor pentatonic scale." We won't violate our philosophy and bog down in theory here, but for the sake of knowing what you're playing, on that 12th fret, the 1st and 6th strings is the note, "E." This serves as the identifying point for this scale; thus, it's "E minor." That's why it's called the "root note fret," because that serves as the "root" of the scale.

So how do we approach this thing? You can't just play random notes all over the pattern; you need some kind of system for visualizing and organizing the pattern. That's the purpose of the five boxes, indicated by the fine gray lines. These are the famous "Pentatonic boxes" you've heard about a million times.

One last point before we actually start playing, and this is very important, because you will carry it with you for the rest of your guitar-playing life: using the little finger, AKA "pinkie" or "4th finger." There are two kinds of guitar players in this world: those who use the left pinkie, and those who don't. Virtually all good players use it, and it makes sense. I mean, good heavens, observe how far apart you can spread your 1st and 3rd fingers, compared to how far you can spread your 1st and 4th! Also, not using the little finger is another bad habit that will take forever to unlearn, if you can at all. If you play for several years without the little finger and then decide to start using it, you'll basically have to learn to play all over again.

Now... turn on your amp, pick up your guitar and hold it in your lap. Here we go! In the first box, hold your forefinger over the 1st fret, your middle finger over the 2nd fret, your ring finger on the 3rd fret, and your pinkie on the 4th fret. See? Four frets, four fingers, nice and neat. One finger per fret.

Keeping the back of your left wrist straight and your fingers relaxed, play the indicated notes in the first box, including the notes on the open strings. Start with the 6th (bass) string and play up to the 1st string, then go back down. Alternate your picking direction; up, down, up, down. It will come naturally; don't worry about it. Just don't play it with all downstrokes or all upstrokes. If you do that, you might as well throw your guitar into the fireplace. Again, and I'm sorry if I sound almost obsessed with this, but *keep your left hand and fingers relaxed*. Watch top players like B.B. King sometime; their fingers are so relaxed, you can hardly tell they're moving. The more tense your hand and fingers are, the worse you will play. Trust me on that one.

For most people, play about 1 note per second. You may be able to play a little faster, but the critically important thing is this: play it only as fast as you can play it smoothly and perfectly. That means smoothly blending each note into the next, without a perceptible break. If you find yourself breaking between notes, with a "beep, beep, blip, blip, beep" sound, *slow down* until you can do it right! Bad habits formed at this stage can become permanent handicaps, and will prevent you from ever playing fast and smoothly like those guitar gods you envy so much. This is why some people play 30 years and still can't play a fast lick: they went too fast as beginners and didn't get down those fundamentals. Don't make this mistake!

Look at the pattern in that first box. Visualize it in your mind. Burn it into your brain. Engrave it into your retinas. Poke it in your mashed potatoes. Everything you learn from now on will be based on your knowledge of these patterns. Whatever works for you, but etch this pattern into your memory, until you can look at the fretboard and instantly see it without even thinking about it.

Now: repeat all of the above with the same box on the 12th fret. This time, the "open string" will be on the 12th fret, so you'll have to finger it. Remember, the pattern always repeats itself at the 12th fret. It's almost like you have two guitars. So, you'll learn each box in two locations.

Now you've gotten started and practiced the first box in both positions, and you can do everything correctly at about 4 notes per second (check your speed with your metronome). Now it's time to move to the second box. Note that in this box, there are no open strings. No more freebies! From now on, you'll have to finger every note, from here all the way to the top of the neck. Remember to use that basic one-finger-per-fret fingering.

As you go through these, you might have noticed something different about the 3rd box: it covers five frets instead of four. So how do you divide that among only four fingers? Like this: play the 2nd and 3rd string notes with the 1st and 4th fingers. Play the rest with the 1st and 3rd fingers. In time you may come up with a different preference.

Practice all of the boxes on the guitar neck, up and down, one after the other, until you can easily visualize and play them, without stopping and thinking, "uh.. where is it?" After you can do that, start skipping to every other box, or just jumping from box to box at random. Get it down pat.

THE SECRET: BREAKING THROUGH!

OK, here we go. It's right about at this stage where beginners start getting bored with practicing, and with the monotony of playing up and down and up and down and up and down the scale. Next thing you know, they're skipping practice sessions, and their guitars are heading for…. the closet. Here's how to break through that "wall" and practice in such a way that it's stimulating and gives you room for some creativity and satisfaction. *It's now or never!*

After you learn a box pattern, you'll spend some time at first just going up and down and up and down the notes, from the 6th string to the 1st string and back. Usually there are about 12 notes, from one end to the other. At first, you'll just play them in order:

1 2 3 4 5 6 7 8 9 10 11 12

Once you get that down pat, go to the next step: play overlapping clusters of notes, like this:

1 2 3   2 3 4   3 4 5   4 5 6   5 6 7 ..... and so on. Then the same thing going back down:

12 11 10   11 10 9   10 9 8   9 8 7 ....

Focus on playing *smoothly,* in one long string, until you can do it without thinking. What will happen eventually is, you'll start playing "out of sequence," making up your own little melodies and rhythms. And there you go! The door is open! Finally, after all these years!!

From there, practice more complex sequences, such as:

1 3 2   2 4 3   3 5 4   4 6 5 ..... and so on, again in both directions, focusing on playing *smoothly,* blending the notes together, and not going "plink, plink, plink." Then, as you get more comfortable with it, maybe you can practice with *longer* sequences:

1 2 3 4 5   2 3 4 5 6   3 4 5 6 7 .... and of course, the note sequences can vary in almost infinite order:

1 2 5 4 3   2 3 6 5 4   3 4 7 6 5 ..... and so on.

Then..... the final step!! *Try NOT playing all the notes at the same tempo.* Play some notes longer or shorter than the others, creating not only a rhythm, but also a *melody*. Trust me, when you start doing this, it's really, really going to be fun.

When you can do this jumping from one box to another without thinking about it, start picking in varying places all over the neck. Pick every other string, every third string. Fret the notes going up one string, down the next. Fret notes all over the pattern at random. Learn to play with some vibrato on certain notes; when you finger the note, slide the fingertip back and forth to give it a wah-wah sound. B.B. King was a master at this. This is why you see the finish worn off of those old Guitar fretboards!

LEVEL TWO: HALF-BOXES

OK, you've practiced these boxes until it's automatic. You can visualize them without pausing and "hunting" for them, and you can jump from one box to another, anywhere on the next, and play the pentatonic notes in it. Now let's go to Level Two: let's move around a little more methodically.

Go to the fourth box and play only the six notes on the first three strings, as shown below. Remember to use all four fingers: four frets, four fingers!

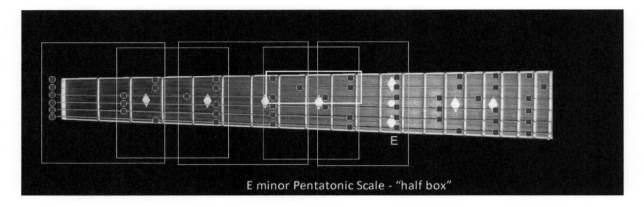

E minor Pentatonic Scale - "half box"

Play the six pentatonic notes in this "half-box" in varying sequences. Play them up, play them down, play them at random. Play them until you can play every imaginable combination of notes in that three-string "half box" without missing a beat.

THE BIG KAHUNA!

Wow, here we are already! You're getting pretty good! Calm down, now. Take a deep breath. This can be a defining moment for many beginners; your first playing that sounds like real music! This may be it! Your big moment! Be sure your metronome or rhythm source is going (as it always should be). Now play a string of 3 to 6 notes. Any notes in the half-box pattern. Now, syncing them with your rhythm source, play them with a specific rhythm. Any rhythm.

As you did at first, repeat this rhythm pattern (or one you made up) all over that half-box, in every possible combination of notes, until you feel like you've covered them all. Try moving your finger back and forth while holding a longer note, creating a vibrato effect. Try hitting a note and sliding your finger down the neck. Play a different set of notes each time. Try playing the first three notes in one box, and the last three in another box.

You get the picture. Come'on! Play! Just let go and play! Let that feeling and emotion *flow* through your fingers! Play! Don't stop! Focus! *Play! Play! Play!* COME'ON, YOU CAN DO IT!!!!!! Make that baby sing!

Whew. Not bad, eh? Take a break. Walk the dog around the block. Go gas up the car.

THE OTHER SIDE

What you just did with that half-box is very, very important, because that's what you're going to do for the next several weeks: break down those 5 boxes into 10 half-boxes. And as you go through this process, your ability to create spontaneous music will accelerate dramatically.

Next, do the exact same thing in the 4th box with the bottom three strings, as outlined below. There are six notes there, as well. Repeat what you did above for the first three strings in the upper half-box.

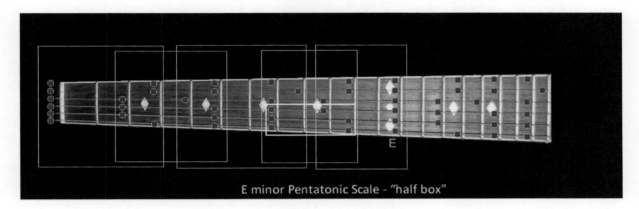

E minor Pentatonic Scale - "half box"

Remember: play those notes, don't just sit there going "duh, duh, duh! Play with a rhythm. Play with a mix of fast, slow, varying melodies. Put that emotion and feeling in them. Enjoy it! Let your guitar be the singing voice of your heart!

So... actually, what you've done is divide the 4th box into two half-boxes. Now it's time for some more serious work: do this for all five boxes, up and down the neck. That gives you ten boxes. This is very important, fundamental work that will form the basis of your playing from this point on. Spend at least a month on it. Practice it until you can smoothly play and jump around those half-boxes like a grasshopper in a hot skillet.

BONUS TIP: this is not part of the approach, but some people really want to dig into this as deeply as they can, so the option is there if you want to take it, but again, you don't have to. The tip is that these two half-boxes are on two groups of strings: the 1st, 2nd, and 3rd, and the 4th, 5th and 6th. But the truth is, there are two other boxes imbedded in that pattern you can utilize as well, if you want to put in the extra time to practice them. Those are the half-boxes on the 2nd, 3rd 4th strings, and then the 3rd, 4th and 5th strings. Again, you don't have to do this. It's just an option which is there for those who are gluttons for punishment and want to push their creative pallettes to the absolute extreme.

Actually, some people just stop right here, being completely satisfied with what we've covered so far. The fact is, you can spend years making all kinds of beautiful music with just what you've learned up to now. But if you're not one of those and you want to further explore the frontiers of your mind, we will now take it all up to the next level. This will add another entire dimension to your creativity.

LEVEL THREE: THE RELATIVE

You've learned the E minor pentatonic scale. The root note (remember?) is the note "E" on the 1st and 12th strings, which is at the 12th fret. Now we're going to introduce the second dimension of this picture: the relative.

Think of these pentatonic scales as always coming in pairs: every pentatonic scale has a identical scale that goes with it, called the relative. You can play in the pentatonic, then the relative, or vice-versa, or mix them together - but let's not get ahead of ourselves. Later, we'll go down that road and learn how to do that. It's very simple and easy, but we're not quite there yet.

Any pentatonic scale's relative scale is three frets lower on the neck. Where the root note for the E minor pentatonic is on the 12th fret, its relative scale is three notes lower: on the 9th fret. Look at the pictures below of the E minor pentatonic we just learned and its relative. Note the location of the root note fret in the relative scale: it's on the 9th fret, compared to the original scale's 12th fret.

Here's the now-familiar E minor Pentatonic:

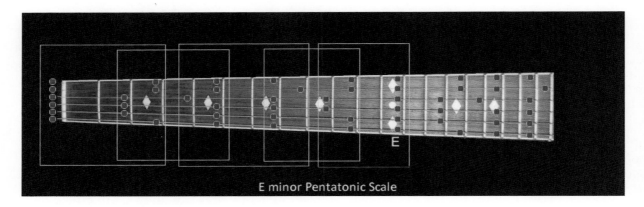

E minor Pentatonic Scale

And here is its Relative. Notice the root note three frets lower, on the 9th fret:

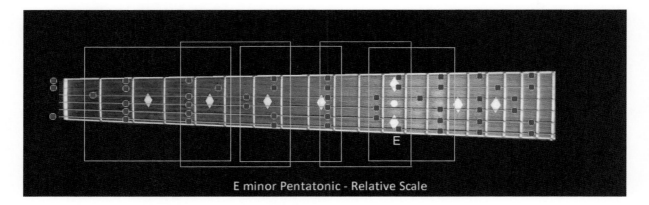

E minor Pentatonic - Relative Scale

Let's study this picture for a minute. Notice how in this relative scale, you have the exact same boxes and patterns; they've all simply shifted down three frets. Notice also how, as with the E, the pattern repeats itself at the 12th fret. Everything is exactly the same, just shifted down three frets from where it was. So basically, you already know how to play this! Surprise!

By the way: this relative scale is actually called the "D-flat minor Pentatonic," because the note on the 1st and 6st strings at the 9th fret is D-flat. So now you've learned two scales: the E minor Pentatonic, and the D-flat minor Pentatonic. When somebody hears you play and asks about it, you can impress the heck out of them by casually saying, "ooooooooooooh, I'm improvising in D-flat minor Pentatonic." It's fun to say that and watch them give you that deer-in-the-headlights stare. Chances are they're some of those that "learned a few basic chords" and know no more about D-flat minor scales than they do about how the Egyptians built the Pyramids.

GROWING UP

No matter how you approach playing the guitar or any other instrument, you've always heard people say "practice, practice, practice." Certainly, the ability to do this is what separates the men from the boys, so to speak. Sure, it's fun to learn new stuff, but there comes a point where to really learn it, you have to roll up your sleeves and do some serious work. But it's not wasted or pointless. This is where you start moving towards being a good player, and opening up vast new horizons for your creativity and expression. This is where you reach that point where you pick a few notes and then start realizing, "hey, I can really play this thing!" And that's what we're going to do here. In a word: go through and practice and learn and practice and learn this relative scale exactly the way you did with the first scale, from start to finish. Do the pattern, the boxes, the half-boxes, everything.

One difference here, though, is that it won't be quite so boring! Now you have some basic knowledge and skill to work with while you're practicing, which will make your practice sessions much more interesting and enjoyable. A typical practice session might consist of:

1. Warm-up
2. E minor pentatonic, random boxes
3. E minor pentatonic, random half-boxes
4. E minor pentatonic, relative, random boxes
5. E minor pentatonic, relative, random half-boxes
6. Relax and play for practice and enjoyment

REGROUPING

Let's stop a minute and look at where we are. If you're reading this, and have been following this approach as presented, you should be a month or two along - maybe three or four - since you started back on Page 1. You've mastered the E minor Pentatonic scale and its Relative. You can visualize both of them all over the neck, as several components: as a whole pattern, divided into boxes, and divided into half-boxes. You've learned to play these components in any sequence or pattern. And most of all, you've learned to use these components to create music, as much as you want, for as long as you want.

As before, many people will just stop right here, completely satisfied with what they've gained. You're certainly welcome to do that. But... if you'd like to keep moving forward, and get even better, take a deep breath and we will go on to another component, this one very different, that will take your playing and enjoyment to yet another whole new level: the concept of "bridgenotes."

LEVEL FOUR: BUILD THE BRIDGE, THEN CROSS IT

Now, let me make it clear that before you step through this door, you must have mastered everything we've talked about up to this point, since you started this process several months ago. If you can confidently say that you have, you're golden. Let's go!

Look again at that E minor Pentatonic:

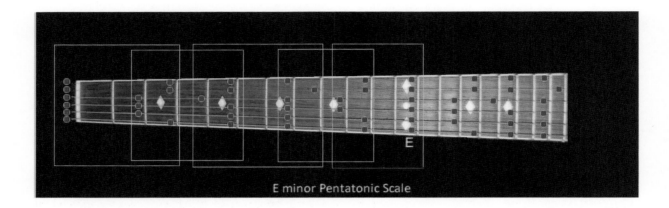

E minor Pentatonic Scale

You can see the pattern on the fretboard. Of course, by now you should be able to visualize it without the "dots."

Now look at its relative:

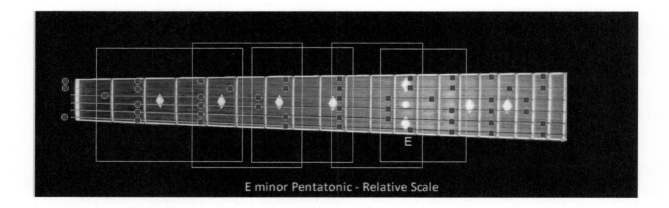

E minor Pentatonic - Relative Scale

As we know, the pattern and the boxes all stay identical; they are just moved down three frets from the original scale. Remember, a pentatonic scale's relative will always be three frets down the neck!

Up until now, we have talked about these two scales separately, focusing on one, then on the other, and sometimes jumping back and forth between the two. Now we're going to do something different, adding another layer to our knowledge. What I'm talking about is the fact that these two scales work together. They are intertwined with each other so that you can combine them into one pattern that will infinitely increase your creative horizons.

Let's start by looking again at the original E minor pentatonic:

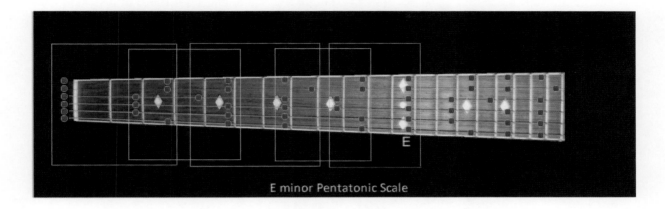

E minor Pentatonic Scale

Now, let's take a big step: let's overlay the relative on top of it. Of course, you won't see some notes because they are shared by both scales. But there are a few that stand out, because they are in the relative scale, but not in the original scale. These notes are indicated by the green dots. These are very important. We will call them bridge notes. Study this picture closely.

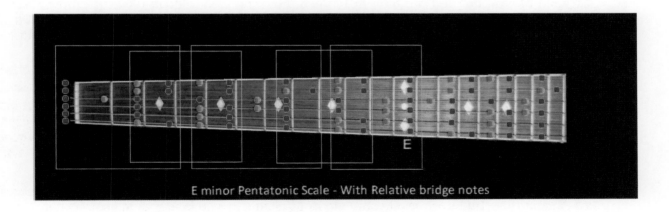

E minor Pentatonic Scale - With Relative bridge notes

The picture above is going to be your guide for the next step in your development as a player. Now it's time to roll up your sleeves again and do a little more work, but this time it will be much easier, since by now you know the patterns instinctively and, because of your ongoing practice, your fingering ability is at a much higher level than it was at the beginning.

What you will do now is go back through the box-by-box practice exactly like you did back when you first started with the E minor Pentatonic. The difference this time will be that you'll be learning a slightly modified pattern: the original E minor Pentatonic plus the additional bridge notes. Don't become overdependent on them. Play in the regular E minor Pentatonic, and just occasionally insert a bridge note, then return to the regular scale. With practice, you will quickly learn how and when to use the bridge notes to vastly enhance the variety, melody and beauty of your playing! Trust me, you'll be thrilled!

Go through the usual practice process - box skipping, string-jumping, the half boxes, etc. just like you did the first time, until you can use the bridge notes without thinking. But one thing is very important here: don't just see this as a single big scale, just with more notes! You must still see yourself as playing the basic E minor Pentatonic scale, using the bridge notes as extra, additional notes that you insert for embellishment. Now read that sentence again; it's very important!

LEVEL FIVE: FLIPPING IT OVER

By now, if you've been following and using this book as you're supposed to, you should be playing some really nice music. You're already better than 99% of the guitar players out there. At this point, you can easily go into a music store and turn heads, or have people gather around when you start playing at a party. And as always, you can stop here if you want, and be happy and proud (and justifiably so!) of what you've accomplished. Just using what you've learned so far, you could spend the rest of your life exploring your fretboard, and enjoying every minute of it!

However ("here he goes again!"): if you so desire, we can move this up yet another step. Now let's flip it over and do the reverse: let's start with the Relative scale, and overlay the original E minor Pentatonic over it! That's just the opposite of what we did last time. But let me warn you: this isn't just another batch of exercises. After you master this, it will open the door to a whole new world of playing, a hundred times bigger than everything you've learned so far! But we'll get into that later.

Let's take another look at that Relative scale:

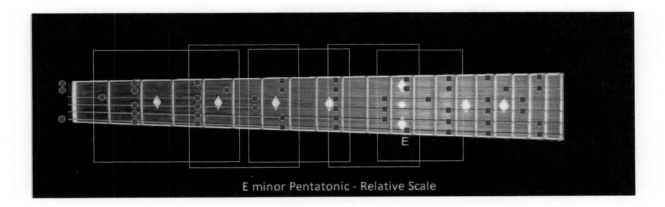

E minor Pentatonic - Relative Scale

And another look at that E minor Pentatonic scale:

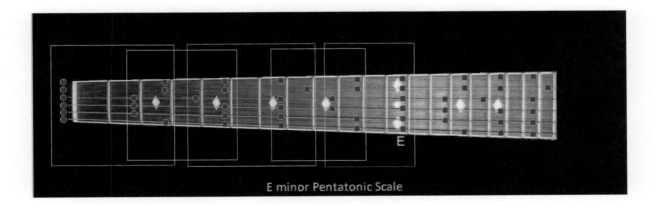

E minor Pentatonic Scale

And now let's overlay the E minor Penatonic on top of that Relative scale:

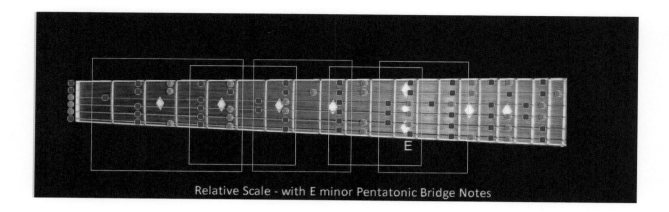

Relative Scale - with E minor Pentatonic Bridge Notes

See how it works? It's just like we had before, only instead of the Relative overlaying the E minor Pentatonic, it's the E minor Pentatonic overlaying the Relative.

By now, you probably know what I'm going to say next: roll up your sleeves and practice! Like the first time, go through the whole process: boxes, skipping, half-boxes, and so on. And remember: again, do not see this as just a different scale with more notes! It's very important that you focus on playing primarily the Relative scale, with the E minor Pentatonic (green) notes as extra, additional notes you insert for effect. OK, see you in a couple of weeks.

CONGRATULATIONS!

If you've made it this far, let me be the first to congratulate you! You have now mastered the process of spontaneously playing on a Pentatonic scale and its Relative. When your friends hear you play, they make comments like, "oh, wow, man, you are good!" You can go into a music store, casually pick a guitar off the rack and start playing, and people will turn and look and smile and nod their heads to your rhythm. Some will even walk over and sit close to you and just enjoy listening to you. But most importantly, you will be able to just play for yourself, any time, any place. You can just pick up a guitar, any guitar, lean back and play, to your heart's content, for hours on end. You made it!

Uh-oh. You probably know what I'm going to say next: "yes, you can go even further..."

LEVEL SIX: CROSSING THE BRIDGES

There's a reason we call those green notes "bridge notes." It's because they serve as "bridges" to help you cross over from one scale to another, e.g. from the E minor Pentatonic to the Relative, and vice- versa.

The use of bridge notes is simple. It works like this: when going from one scale to the other (i.e. the original to the Relative, or the Relative to the original), play one of the bridge notes in between. That's it. If you're playing basically in E minor Pentatonic and you want to change to playing based in its Relative, use a bridge note as a sort of "connection" or... well... a "bridge" between the two scales. Easy enough? OK, roll your sleeves back up and have at it.

LEVEL SEVEN: HORIZONS BEYOND THE HORIZON

So far, everything you've seen has been in the "Key of E" - the E minor Pentatonic and its Relative. Now that you've mastered that, you may want to start exploring other keys. But before you do, remember that no matter what key you're playing in, everything is identical to what you've learned so far. Every key will exact same boxes, exact same patterns, exact same everything The only difference is that key's position on the neck!

Now you understand why it was so important to learn to play those patterns until they were ingrained into your subconcious: because when you start going to other keys, you'll already know how to play them!

For now, the sequence of keys you should learn should follow the sequence of notes going across the guitar strings: E, A, D, G, B, E. You've mastered E, so next you can move to A. Again, it's all exactly the same. Your basic scale will be A minor Pentatonic, and its Relative will be three frets lower. Remember, same boxes, same patterns, same everything.

We won't look at every single one of these scales, but let's go ahead and take a look at A minor Pentatonic. Like the E's root was on the 12th fret, A's root is on the 5th fret. So the A minor Pentatonic, its relative, and both scales with their bridge notes will look like this:

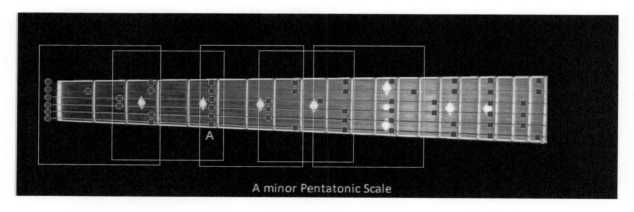

A minor Pentatonic Scale

First, the base A minor Pentatonic. Root is on the 5th fret. See that familiar pattern? Then its Relative, down three frets to the 2nd fret:

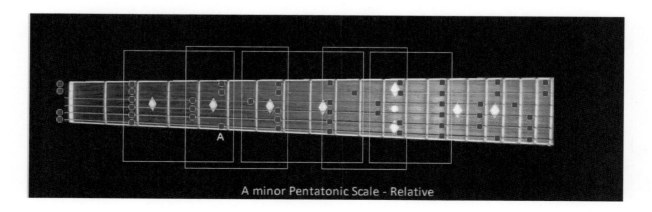

A minor Pentatonic Scale - Relative

Then the A minor Pentatonic with the Relative bridge notes. That is, the A minor Pentatonic with the Relative "laid on top of it":

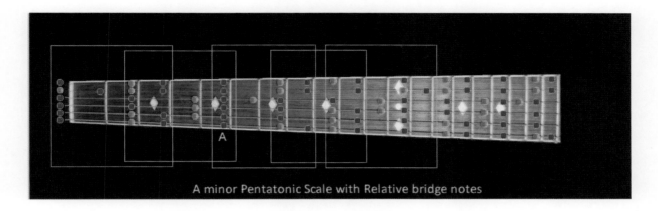

A minor Pentatonic Scale with Relative bridge notes

And last, the Relative, with the A minor Pentatonic overlaying it:

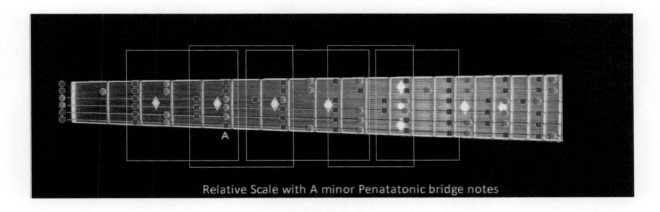

Relative Scale with A minor Penatatonic bridge notes

Then it goes on to the D minor Pentatonic. Its root is at the 10th fret, and of course its Relative is at the 7th fret.

Next is G minor Pentatonic. Root at the 3rd/15th, Relative at 0 and 12 (yes, you're right! G minor Pentatonic's Relative is the same as E minor Pentatonic!)

Then there is B minor Pentatonic. Root at 7th, Relative at the 4th.

Next is E. What? E? Haven't we....? Congratulations! You've gone full circle!

To help you visualize where these roots are and to sort of sew everything up, here are all the root note frets:

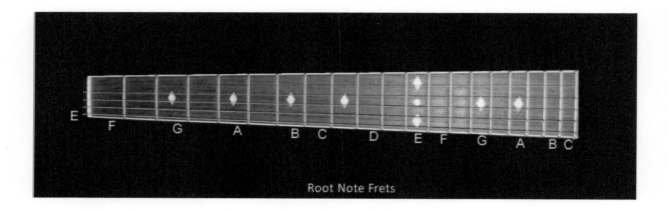

Root Note Frets

That pretty well wraps it up. Ultimately, if you stay with it, you will be able to work with this Penta-tonic/Relative duality for every single root on the neck, and move around them with ease.

A FEW FAREWELL NOTES

Remember always to play with rhythm and melody, don't just sit there going duh, duh, duh, back and forth across the strings, up and down the box.

By now you also might have started using some slides and bends, and maybe hammer-ons and pull-offs. We're not going to get into these techniques here, simply because there is a huge amount of information on them already out there. Dive in whenever you want.

If you've really followed this book line by line and done everything it says to do, you're a few months away from when you started on Page 1. You've come a long way! You can play all kinds of music, smoothly and confidently, slow and fast. When you pick up a guitar in a music store or at a party, everybody turns and listens. If you're over at a friend's house and pick a little on his guitar, people with stop talking and gather around. And most importantly, you can play for your own pleasure, any time, any place, for hours at a time. And you did it all without learning one... single... chord.

Listen to music all you can. Vocal and instrumental, slow and fast, new and old, every style. Play different guitars. Experiment with different effects pedals, different strings, picks, amplifiers. And if you're so inclined, start learning some chords, sightreading and music theory. It will make a lot of things fall into place.

But no matter what you do, never, *never* quit learning and exploring the infinite universe of music out there. Go where your heart yearns to go, and *never* let anybody else tell you differently. Now, go get your guitar and *play*!

- Ron Prellop

Printed in Great Britain
by Amazon

28637353R00023